Sphinx Theatre Company
Presents

A Wedding Story
by Bryony Lavery

Originally co-produced with
Birmingham Repertory Theatre

Opened at the door, Birmingham
Repertory Theatre 2 November
2000

First London performance
Soho Theatre
16 January 2001

Sphinx Theatre Company is
sponsored by Gander & White

THE REP
Birmingham Repertory Theatre

THE ARTS COUNCIL OF ENGLAND

sphinx

Sphinx has played a proud and historic role in British theatre over the past 27 years. Supported by the Arts Council of England since 1973, it has toured nationally and internationally, specialising in producing new work by established women artists. There is scarcely a woman writer writing in the theatre today who has not worked with the company, or who has not been touched by its pioneering activities.

Most recent productions:
Sweet Dreams by Diane Esguerra, a dramatic interpretation of Freud's Case History of Dora.
Sweet Dreams was first produced in association with the Chelsea Centre, London in October 1999, and the production then toured England in May - June 2000. This provocative play generated huge interest from critics and audiences alike. Sphinx also organised a series of debates to coincide with the production, in which prominent psychoanalysts and academics put 'Freud on the Couch'.

Vita & Virginia by Eileen Atkins, adapted from the correspondence between Virginia Woolf and Vita Sackville-West, directed by Maria Aitken.
Vita & Virginia was a co-production with Watford Palace Theatre. This elegant, visually enchanting production toured nationally in February - March 1999 before opening at Watford Palace Theatre in April 1999.

Commissioned writers: Pam Gems, Claire Luckham, Timberlake Wertenbaker.

Sphinx Theatre Company are presenting:

Cherished Disappointments In Love
By Jouko and Juha Turkka
Adapted from the Finnish by Bryony Lavery

At the Soho Theatre, London from 12 September – 6 October

Directed by Sue Parrish

Cast: Janet Suzman, Les Dennis, Nicky Ladanowski, Esa-Matti Pölhö

For tickets and information please call 020 7478 0100

Sue Parrish
Producer, Sphinx Theatre Company

Amanda Rigali
General Manager, Sphinx Theatre Company

Alison Ritchie
Production Manager for Sphinx

Mark Slaughter
Press & Marketing Consultant for Sphinx

Sphinx Theatre Company
25 Short St
London SE1 8LJ
Tel: 0207 401 9993
Fax: 0207 401 9995

A Wedding Story is Sphinx Theatre Company's first co-production with Birmingham Repertory Theatre

sphinx

A Wedding Story
by Bryony Lavery

Sally
Abigail Hercules

Peter
Andrew Hawkins

Robin
Matthew Bose

Grace
Nancy Crane

Evelyn
Kika Markham

Writer
Bryony Lavery

Director
Annie Castledine

Designer
Ruari Murchison

Lighting Designer
Nick Beadle

Composer
Timothy Sutton

Staff Director
Janette Smith

Stage Manager
Jamie Byron

Technical Stage Manager
Neil Gavin

Production Credits

Trophy Supplied by
**John Bull supporting
The Best Of British**

Sainsbury's

Biographies

sphinx

Nancy Crane
Grace

Theatre: *Six Degrees of Separation* (Sheffield Crucible); *Our Late Night* (Royal Court); *Absolution* (BAC); *The Strip* (Royal Court); *Angels in America* and *Millennium Approaches* (RNT); Threesome (Gay Sweatshop); *Last of the Red Hot Lovers* (Derby Playhouse).

TV: *Strike Force; Last Days of Patton; 92 Grosvenor Street.*

Film: *The Fourth Protocol.*

Radio: *The Brutality of Fact; Open Secrets; What Makes Sammy Run; The Affair at Grover Station; The Country; The Strip; Alaska* (all for the BBC).

Andrew Hawkins
Peter

Theatre: Samuel Pepys in *A Passionate Englishman* (City of London Festival 2000); Albany in *King Lear* (Manchester Royal Exchange); other repertory at Bristol, Edinburgh, Ipswich, Colchester and Watford including Macheath in *The Threepenny Opera; French Without Tears; Small Change; David Copperfield; The Alchemist; Confusions; Henry V; Plunder; Edward II; The Complaisant Lover.* With the RSC, *Baal; The Suicide; Pericles; Julius Caesar; The Knight of the Burning Pestle;* and the original production of *Nicholas Nickleby* at the Aldwych Theatre and on Broadway. At the Lyric Hammersmith, *The Cenci* by Shelley and *Katerina* by Andreyev. Tours and West End: *The Clandestine Marriage; Married Love; Time and The Conways* (Old Vic), which also toured Canada. Chichester Festival: *Patriot for Me* and *Time and The Conways; The House of Mirth* (Cambridge Theatre Company) directed by Annie Castledine.

TV: *The Glittering Prizes; Good Behaviour; Strange But True; Making News; The Black Tower; Napoleon and Josephine; Nicholas Nickleby; Bugs; Moving Story; Citizen Locke; Hearbeat; Bliss.*

Film: *Chariots of Fire; The Whistleblower; Top Secret; The Object of Beauty; The Son of the Pink Panther; Shadowlands; Tomorrow Never Dies.*

Andrew has also worked as a director in UK and the USA, and with students at RADA, the Drama Centre, and other London academies.

Mathew Bose
Robin

Abigail Hercules
Sally

Training: LAMDA

Theatre: *East is East* (Leicester Haymarket); *Song at Twilight* (West End); *Lulu* (Canal Café); *Scapin* and *Progress* (Lion and Unicorn); *Little Pictures* (Los Angeles Theatre Centre).

TV: *The Mullet Chronicles (and internet)*; *Coupling*; *Doc Marten*; *My Family*.

Film: *American Mullet; Angel; Uncommon Ground; The Dinner Guest; Murder by Numbers; I Need You; Going Down.*

Theatre: T*he Ghosts of Poe* (Tour de Force); *Miss Dis'Grace* (Riverside Studios); Hunky Dory (Oily Cart); *Ti fr* (BFT); Buddy (National Tour); *Yerma* (BAC); *Calamity Jane* (BAC); *Black Coffee* (National Tour); *Le Grand Meaulnes* (Young Vic); *Grease* (Young Vic).

Film: *Dinner Money.*

Biographies

Kika Markham
Evelyn

Training:
Guildhall School
of Music and
Drama

Theatre: Harriet in *Shelly* by Ann Jellicoe; Abigail in *Time Present* by John Osborne; Viola in *Twelfth Night* at The Royal Court Theatre. Kika has twice played Anna Akhmatova, The Russian Poet, once in Maureen Lawrence's *Real Writing* directed by her husband Corin Redgrave and in *Black Sail, White Sail* by Helene Cixous directed by Sue Parrish at The Gate Theatre. Two plays by Tony Kushner, Agnes in *A Bright Room Called Day* (Bush Theatre) and *Home Body/Kabul* a new play that he wrote for her. This April Kika won an Olivier Nomination and Clarence Derwent Award for Best Supporting Actress as Hilde Latymer in *Song at Twilight* by Noël Coward. She has worked previously with Annie Castledine in *The Country Girl*, Greenwich Theatre. She has recently appeared in *The Vagina Monologues* in the West End.

TV: *Black Silk* series with Rudolph William (BBC 2); *Clouds of Glory* (Granada); *Edward & Mrs Simpson* (Thames); *Poirot* (LWT); *Cracker* (Granada); *Double Dare* (BBC); *Blade on the Feather* Dennis Potter (LWT); *Taking Over the Asylum* (BBC2); *Kavanagh QC* (Carlton); *Touching Evil* (ITV); *Trial and Retribution IV* by Lynda La Plante playing Mrs Justice Piggot.

Radio: Daisy in *Roz and Daisy* by Corin Redgrave

Film: Carol in *A Very British Coup*, Mick Jackson; Anne in *Deux Anglaisis* and le Continent, Francois Truffaut. *Outlander* with Sean Connery;. Eileen in *Wonderland* directed by Michael Winterbottom; Trish in *Esther Khan* with Summer Phoenix and Ian Holm, directed by Arnaud Desplechin released in December. She starts filming *Killing Me Softly* in Spring 2001.

Bryony Lavery
Writer

Bryony Lavery's plays include *Helen and Her Friends* (1978); *Bag* (1979); *The Family Album* (1980); *Calamity* (1983); *Origin of The Species* (1984); *Witchcraze* (1985); *Her Aching Heart* (Pink Paper Play of The Year 1991); *Kitchen Matters* (1990); *Nothing Compares to You* (Produced at The Rep in 1995); *Ophelia* (1996); *Goliath* (1997) and *Frozen* (Produced at The Rep in 1998) which won both the TMA Best New Play 1998 and the Eileen Anderson Central Television Award for Best Play 1998.

For five years Bryony was Artistic Director of Les Oeufs Malades. She was joint Artistic Director of Gay Sweatshop from 1989-1991 and a Tutor in Playwriting on the MA Playwriting Course at Birmingham University for three years.

She was Resident Playwright at the Unicorn Theatre for Children, 1986-7 and her work for children includes *The Zulu Hut Club* (1983); *Sore Points* (1985); *Madagascar* (1987); *The Dragon Wakes* (1988) and *Down Among The Minibeasts* (1996), which was nominated for Best Children's Play Writers Guild Awards 1996. Her cabaret work includes *Time Gentleman Please* (1978); *Female Trouble* (1981); *More Female Trouble* (1982); *The Wandsworth Warmers* (1984). She has appeared in all five of the legendary Drill Hall pantomimes and co-written two of them, *Peter Pan* (1991) and *The Sleeping Beauty* (1992).

Her extensive work for BBC includes the groundbreaking *Revolting Women* for BBC2, adaptations of *Wuthering Heights, Lady Audley's Secret* and *A High Wind* in Jamaica for the Classic Serial, and original plays *The Smell of Him, The Twelve Days of Christmas, Velma and Therese, No Joan of Arc* and *Woman of Ice* for Radio 4.

Recent Work includes *Shot Through The Heart*, a site-specific large-cast multi-media piece performed at Ludlow Castle, Shropshire July 2000; *Illyria*, a new play which opened August 2000 at ACT in San Francisco, and an adaptation of *Behind the Scenes at the Museum* for BBC Radio 4. Her biography of Tallulah Bankhead was published in 1999 and her play *More Light* is published in October 2000.

She is currently working on *The Opera Companion* for Salisbury Playhouse, *The Easter Parade* for Birmingham Rep and *Smoke* for The New Victoria

Theatre, Stoke-on-Trent. She is writing an English version of the the Finnish play *Cherished Disappointments in Love*, by Jouha Tourka, for Sphinx. She is developing a film *Who Killed Josie O'Dwyer?* and a series *Girls* for television. Her adaptation of Kate Atkinson's *Behind the Scenes at the Museum* opened at York Theatre Royal in October. Her adaptation of Kate Atkinson's Behind the Scenes at the Museum opened at York Theatre Royal in October. Her adaptation of Angela Carter's *The Magic Toyshop* is being produced by Shared Experience Theatre this year for a national tour.

She is Honorary Doctor of Arts at De Montfort University.

Biographies

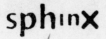

Annie Castledine
Director

Annie Castledine was Artistic Director of Derby Playhouse from 1987 to 1990, a historic period for Regional Repertory Theatres. Since then she has worked as a freelance theatre director in theatres all over the country and in radio and television.

This year her work includes *Spoonface Steinberg* by Lee Hall, co-directed with Marcello Magni and Kathryn Hunter at The New Ambassador's Theatre, and *Marie* by Steve Trafford performed by Elizabeth Mansfield in the first tour by their production company, Visiting Moon Productions. She also directed *The Gift* by Roy Williams for Birmingham Repertory Theatre and *The Life and Death of Marilyn Monroe* by Gerlind Reinshagen at the Royal National Theatre Studio in June.
In July and August 2000 Annie directed two pieces for radio, *Autumn Sonata* by Ingmar Bergman for Radio 3 and a new play by Mark Wheatley for Radio 4.

In 2001 Annie Castledine has directed Brecht's *The Mother* for Visiting Moon productions, which tiured nationally. She has directed the first adaptation of a Raymond Carver short story by Mark Wheatley for radio 4, produced by Catherine Bailey Ltd. *Spoonface Steinberg* will be seen in the Linoln centre as part of a world tour.

Sue Parrish
Producer

Sue Parrish is Artistic Director of Sphinx Theatre Company, and Producer for Sphinx of A *Wedding Story*. Sue produced for the Company *Goliath* by Bryony Lavery, directed by Annie Castledine, *The Snow Palace* by Pam Gems, directed by Janet Suzman, and *Vita & Virginia* by Eileen Atkins, directed by Maria Aitken. Sue has also produced Sphinx's popular Glass Ceiling events since 1991.Sue Parrish's most recent directing credits include *Sweet Dreams* by Diane Esguerra for Sphinx, and *Hamlet* for the City of London Festival.

She is currently directing *Cherished Disappointments in Love*, adapted from the Finnish by Bryony Lavery, which will open at the Soho Theatre in September 2001.

Ruari Murchison
Designer

Ruari has worked in major regional theatres including Nottingham Playhouse, Crucible Theatre Sheffield, West Yorkshire Playhouse, Birmingham Repertory Theatre, Theatr Clwyd and Bristol Old Vic. London work includes productions at the Royal Opera House, Royal National Theatre, Royal Court, Young Vic, Hampstead Theatre Club, Greenwich, Sadlers Wells at the Peacock Theatre and the Lyric Theatre, Shaftsbury Avenue.

Recent design work includes: *Twelfth Night; Hamlet* (Birmingham Repertory Theatre and national tour); *A Busy Day* (Lyric Theatre, Shaftsbury Avenue); *The Waiting Room* and *The Red Balloon* (Royal National Theatre); *The Snowman* (Sadlers Wells at the Peacock Theatre); *The Tempest; Macbeth, The Merchant of Venice, Frozen, Jumpers, Nativity* and *Quarantine* (Birmingham Repertory Theatre); *West Side Story* (Stratford Festival, Canada); *God and Stephen Hawkin* (Bath Theatre Royal).

Opera work includes: Peter Grimes, *Cosi fan Tutte* (Luzerner Opera); *La Cenerentola, Il Barbiere di Siviglia* (Garsington); *L'Italiana in Algeri* (Buxton); *Les Pelerins de la Mecque, ZaZa* (Wexford); *The Magic Flute, A Midsummer Night's Dream* (Covent Garden Festival).

Ballet work includes: *The Protecting Veil* (Birmingham Royal Ballet); *Le Festin de l'Araignée* (Royal Ballet School - Royal Opera House Gala); *Landschaft und Erinnerung* (Stuttgart Ballett) all choreographed by David Bintley.Film work includes: *The Snowman* and *Jean* starring Susannah York (Elysian Films).

Nick Beadle
Lighting Designer

Recent designs include: *The Gift* (Birmingham Repertory Theatre); *Busy Day* (Lyric Hammersmith); *The Guardsman* (Albery Theatre); *Streetcar Named Desire* (Bristol Old Vic); *Hosts of Rebecca, Happy End, Song of the Earth, Art, The Devils, The Rose Tattoo, The Rape of the Fair Country, Dick Whittington, Sweeney Todd and Threepenny Opera* (Clwyd Theatr Cymru), *China Song* (Clear Day Productions Tour and Plymouth Theatre Royal), *A Busy Day* (Bristol Old Vic), *Vita & Virginia* (Sphinx), *Angels Rave On* (Nottingham), *The Alchemical Wedding, Romeo and Juliet, The Cherry Orchard* and *Racing Demon, The Rehearsal* and *The Double Inconstancy* (Salisbury), *The Life of Galileo, The Resistible Rise of Arturo Ui, The Herbal Bed* and *Arcadia* (Library Theatre), Killing Time (National Tour), *Shirley Valentine* (National Tour), *Suzanna Andler* and *Hedda Garbler* (Chichester and Tour), *Vertigo* (Guilford), *Watching the Sand by the Sea* (Derby), *Tosca* (Opera Holland Park) and *The Marriage of Figaro* (English Touring Opera). *Canterbury Tales* (Garrick), *Old Times* (Wyndham's), *From The Mississippi Delta* and *Full Moon* (Young Vic), *Jane Eyre* (Playhouse), *Lady Audley's Secret* and *The Broken Heart* (Lyric Hammersmith), *A Midsummer Night's Dream* and *The Tempest* (City of London Festival), *Gaslight, The Piggy Bank, A Country Girl* and *Marie Lloyd* (Greenwich), *A Better Day* and *Waiting to Inhale* (Theatre Royal Stratford East), *Hymn to Love - Homage to Piaf* (Drill Hall), *Women of Troy* (Royal National Theatre).

Biographies

sphinx

Timothy Sutton
Music

Timothy was the assistant conductor of Simon Callow's recent revival of *The Pajama Game* (Birmingham Repertory, Victoria Palace). He has written three musicals, *Beauty and the Beast* which won Best Musical, Vivian Ellis Prize 1990, *Civilisation*, and *Oak*.

Musical direction includes: *Marat/Sade* (Royal National Theatre); *Hymn to Love* (Mercury Colchester, Drill Hall, Traverse Edinburgh and BBC Radio 3); *Killing Rasputin* (Bridewell Theatre); *China Song* (Plymouth Drum and touring); *Marie* (Basingstoke, Keswick and touring); *The Mikado* (Newcastle-under-Lyme). He is currently Assistant Conductor of the D'Oyly Carte's national tour of *HMS Pinafore*.

Incidental music includes: *A Fool and His Money* (Nottingham Playhouse, Birmingham Repertory Theatre) and *The Gift* (Birmingham Repertory Theatre, Tricycle Theatre)

Timothy works closely with director Annie Castledine and Visiting Moon Productions and was Musical Director of *The Mother*, which the company toured in early 2001.

Janette Smith
Staff Director

Janette began her directing career running her own physical theatre company, Moor Theatre in 1995. In 1997 she was winner of the Regional Theatre Young Director's Scheme - resulting in an eighteen month bursary at the Royal Court Theatre. She then became Artistic Director of Camden Young People's Theatre (1999-2000).

Work includes: *The Dove* (Warehouse Theatre), *Rock-a-bye Camden* (Embassy Studio), *No Limits* (The Dome), *Glowing Manikin* (The Actors Centre), *Voices of the Fallen* (New End Theatre), *Trade* (Royal Court Theatre), *Diary of a Madman* (Etcetera Theatre), *Live Punch and Judy* (tour), *Time Lords* (tour), *Bloody Poetry* (White Bear), *Wildsea-Wildsea* (Man in the Moon).

sphinx

Sphinx Past Productions

1973	*Instrument for Love* by Jennifer Phillips
	The Amiable Courtship of Miz Venus and Wild Bill by Pam Gems
	Lovefood by Dinah Brook
	Mal de Mere by Micheline Wandor
	Parade of Cats by Jane Wibberly
1974	*Fantasia* by the company
1975/6	*My Mother Says I Never Should* by the company
1976/7	*Work to Role* by the Company
1977	*Out on the Costa del Trico* by the company
1977/8	*Pretty Ugly* by the company
	In Our Way by the company
1978/9	*Hot Spot* by Eileen Fairweather and Melissa Murray
1978	*Soap Opera* by Donna Franceschild
1979/80	*The Wild Bunch* by Bryony Lavery
1979	*My Mkinga* by the company
1980/1	*Better a Live Pompey than a Dead Cyril* by Claire McIntyre & Stephanie Nunn
	Breaking Through by Timberlake Wertenbaker
1981	*New Anatomies* by Timberlake Wertenbaker
1982	*Time Pieces* by Lou Wakefield and the company
	Double Vision by Libby Mason
1983	*Love and Dissent* by Elisabeth Bond
	Dear Girl by Libby Mason and Tierl Thompson
1984	*Trade Secrets* by Jacqui Shapiro
1984/5	*Pax* by Deborah Levy
1985	*Anywhere to Anywhere* by Joyce Halliday
	Witchcraze by Bryony Lavery
1986	*Fixed Deal* by Paulette Randall
	Our Lady by Deborah Levy
1987	*Holding the Reins* by the company
	Lear's Daughters by Elaine Feinstein, with the company
1988	*Picture Palace* by Winsome Pinnock
1989	*Pinchdice & Co.* by Julie Wilkinson
	Zerri's Choice by Sandra Yaw
1990	*Mortal* by Maro Green and Caroline Griffin
	Her Aching Heart by Bryony Lavery
1990	*Christmas Without Herods* by Lisa Evans
1992	*The Roaring Girl's Hamlet* by Shakespeare, in a setting by Claire Luckham
1992/3	*Every Bit Of It* by Jackie Kay
1993	*Playhouse Creatures* by April De Angelis
1994	*Chandralekha* by Amrit Wilson
	Black Sail White Sail by Helene Cixous

1995	*Hanjo by Seami*, adapted by Diane Esguerra and Yukio Mishima, trans. Donald Keene
1996	*Voyage in the Dark* by Jean Rhys, adapted by Joan Wiles
1997	*Goliath* by Bryony Lavery based on the book by Beatrix Campbell
	Nichola McAuliffe nominated for TMA / Barclays Best Actress Award 1997
1998	*The Snow Palace* by Pam Gems
	Nominated for TMA / Barclays Best Touring Production Award 1998
1999	*Vita & Virginia* by Eileen Atkins, based on the correspondence of Virginia Woolf and Vita Sackville-West
1999 / 2000	*Sweet Dreams* by Diane Esguerra
2000 / 01	*A Wedding Story* by Bryony Lavery
2001	*Cherished Disappointments in Love* adapted from the Finnish by Bryony Lavery

Glass Ceilings

Sphinx's regular event about women in the arts.

1991 at the ICA with Professor Janet Todd, Dr Juliet Dusinberre, Sue Parrish (Chair); Fiona Shaw, Charlotte Keatley, Jill Tweedie and Jenni Murray (Chair).

1992 at the ICA with Hélène Cixous, Sarah Cornell, and Sue Parrish (Chair); Janet Suzman, Deborah Warner, Fiona Shaw, Jackie Kay, and Jenni Murray (Chair).

1993 at the Royal National Theatre with Beatrix Campbell, Susie Orbach and Sue Parrish (Chair); Jude Kelly (Chair), Hélène Cixous, Viv Gardner, Juliet Stephenson, Rona Munro and Di Trevis.

1994 at the Royal National Theatre with Helena Kennedy QC (Chair), Amrit Wilson, Taslima Nasrin and Irina Ratushinskaya; Ruth MacKenzie (Chair), Beatrix Campbell, Jude Kelly, Phyllis Nagy, and Judith Jacob.

1995 at the Royal National Theatre with Sarah Dunant (Chair), Professor Susan Bassnett and Della Grace; Ruth Mackenzie (Chair), Claire Armitstead, Annie Castledine, Kay Mellor, Toyah Willcox and Denise Wong.

1996 at the Royal National Theatre with Germaine Greer, Juliet Mitchell and Dr Lizbeth Goodman (Chair); Jude Kelly (Chair), Annie Castlediine, Pam Gems, Bonnie Greer, Sarah Kane, and Mel Kenyon.

1997 at the Almeida Theatre with Professor Lisa Jardine, Joan Bakewell; Nicholas de Jongh, Mike Phillips, Genista McIntosh (Chair), Beatrix Campbell, Kathryn Hunter, Fiona Shaw, Desmond Barrit and Burt Caesar.

2001 at the Royal National Theatre with Beatrix Campbell; Nancy Lindisfarne; Professor Juliet Mitchell; Professor Lawrence Senelick; Professor Sara Diamond; Helena Goldwater; Dr Lizbeth Goodman; Bonnie Greer and Bryony Lavery.

Bryony Lavery
A Wedding Story

ff

faber and faber

First published in 2000
by Faber and Faber Limited
3 Queen Square, London WC1N 3AU
Published in the United States by Faber and Faber Inc.
an affiliate of Farrar, Straus and Giroux Inc., New York

Typeset by Country Setting, Kingsdown, Kent CT14 8ES
Printed in England by Mackays of Chatham plc

A CIP record for this book
is available from the British Library

ISBN 0–571–20906–8

Characters

Evelyn, a married woman

Peter, a husband

Sally, a daughter

Grace, a woman in love

Robin, a son

Author's Note

This play is laid out to help the actors find
the true rhythms of dramatic speech.

None of the characters speak in sentences
or observe punctuation or breathe at the right time.

Because   often
They are in   torment.

The short lines, the spaces within or between lines,
are there on purpose to indicate the subtext and
to help the performer to find the physical
and emotional journey within a speech.

I hope the reader will observe the deliberate
eccentricities of my punctuation . . .

ONE
A GOOD LAUGH

We are in fog.

In it, a room of today hangs expectant.

Preparations for a small wedding. Clothes, shoes, hats, gifts. A water source.

Our characters appear and disappear in the partnership between light and fog.

The dramatic, introductory music to Casablanca *plays as we see . . .*

Evelyn watching television . . . Casablanca . . . very focused . . . as if studying it . . .

Casablanca
    'With the coming of the second world war
    many eyes in imprisoned Europe
    turned hopefully, or desperately,
    t'ward the freedom of the Americas . . .
    Lisbon became the great embarcation point . . .
    but not everybody could get to Lisbon directly . . .
    and so a tortuous roundabout refugee trail sprang up
    Paris to Marseilles
    across the Mediterranean to Oran
    then by train, or auto, or foot
    across the rim of Africa
    to Casablanca in French Morocco
    here the fortunate ones, through money
    or influence, or luck
    might obtain exit veez-ays
    and scurry to Lisbon
    and from Lisbon to the New World
    but the others wait in Casablanca

and wait
and wait

and wait . . .

Throughout this, Evelyn . . .

Evelyn (*watches intently. Then . . .*)

oh!

It is something she recognises . . .

ah!

She points an oldish finger at what she recognises . . .

ah!

There is something very interesting and nice there . . .
She smiles.

ha.

She watches intently, a smile on her face. Her eyes
move with her head as she watches different details in
all parts of the screen . . .

hmmm.

mmmm.

mmmmmmmm.

The smile broadens. She points again . . . this time
particularly . . . at some detail which makes her
laugh . . .

ha!   ha!

The detail continues to amuse her.
    She laughs delightedly and delightfully for a long
time at what is going on on the screen.
    She is completely amused and in absolute hilarity.

6

ha ha ha ha ha ha ha!

Tears roll down her cheeks and she wipes them away, still laughing.

ha ha ha   (*sniff*)   hhaaaa haaaaa . . .
haahaahaaa . . . (*wipe*)

Somewhere near, someone arrives.

oh!

She has heard. It is very perturbing, unexpected. Her face is completely anxious . . .

Nearer this time . . . another sound only she hears . . . approaching, until . . .

Peter, semi-smartly dressed in a suit, the wrong shoes, enters . . .

Evelyn (*with a joy equal to that for the video*)
ah!

They kiss, embrace . . . this is the great romance . . . as . . .

Peter
You should have come, darling!
You would have loved it!
I'm a little the worse for the drink . . .

He is quite drunk . . .

so much photographing and videoing
to get through we didn't sit down to the *Tuck*
until three so Bucks Fizz and then just Fizz
then just Bucks
and then the father of the girl who
married the *other* brother with the small
catering business who could have
banged out a *much* better three course

deal if they'd come to *him* bought me a
Beer
and then we saw *Draught* Guinness and
Beer and . . .
But what a *magnificent* wedding!
Everybody asked after you . . .
I was a little late . . .
big pile-up on the M-something . . .
took a clever little detour . . .
then the bloody map didn't fit the roads! . . .
arrived just at the 'Do you, Michael,
take thee, Charlotte . . .' stage . . . Evelyn . . .
they were videoing the whole bangshoot
in the church!
What's it all coming to?
. . . I mean, is that allowed, ecclestiastically?
. . . ?
well, *must* be . . .
vicar moving into shot . . .
it's all a bit fly-on-the-pulpit for me but . . .
I oozed into a pew doorside of it all . . .
luckily the *correct* side . . . *our* side, darling . . .
so . . . a lot of 'vaguely marriage' clothes . . .
flung-together outfits . . .
lots of loose tickets in sort-of-smart
and 'oh-they'll-do' shoes

Peter looks at his own 'they'll do' shoes.

Evelyn

Tut tut tut! (*They won't do for her.*)

Peter

I know I know . . . but *this*

He demonstrates his bizarre outfit.

how-d'you-do was right at home!

Evelyn picks confetti off his clothes . . . straightens . . .
as . . .

Their side   spanking new
money had been *spent*
money was *no* object . . .
bridesmaids in peacock blue
pages . . . a sort of mini-Press Gang from
Nelson's bloody navy type of thing! I mean!
Groom and the men and whatnot
dressed as the the Ascot scene from
the *Pygmalion* film . . . (*Snaps his fingers until:*)
. . . *My Fair Lady*!!!!!
And . . .
I've never seen so many bridesmaids and
pages and
babies
wrapped up like lamb chops outside
a Royal Wedding . . .
a child hiccuped throughout . . .

Evelyn
   Ha.

Peter
   you know when you get hiccups . . .?

Both really do know how she gets hiccups . . .

Peter
   Louder than you . . . church very good acoustics . . .
   it hiccuped right through the vows,
   several prayers
   and 'Love Divine'
   stopped only by the Vicar's Address . . .
   whose speciality is clearly . . . *jokes*!!!
   Did . . . 'the bride looks at the church . . .
   she sees . . .

9

He acts this out.

the *aisle* . . .
the *altar* . . .
the *hymn* . . .

Peter
 aisle
 altar
 hymn . . .

 "*I'll alter him*!"
 she thinks!'

Evelyn
 'I'll alter him!'

She laughs delightedly. So does Peter . . . then . . .

Peter
 Very pleased our daughter was behaving herself
 at this . . .
 just kept her head down . . .
 looked . . . *quietly ironic* . . .!

Both Peter and Evelyn react similarly to this . . .

 and then . . .
 outside the church for *more* photo
 opportunities . . .
 I'm taking a photograph of the bride and bridesmaids
 at the gate . . .
 and I think . . . 'Hey, wait a minute . . .
 the bridesmaids were
 in peacock blue and now they're in eau de nil . . .
 and . . . I realise
 I'm photographing the *next wedding*!

*Peter laughs out loud . . . spluttering . . . Evelyn
laughs delightedly too . . .*

Evelyn
   Ha ha ha ha ha!

Peter
   I apologise with unctuous charm . . . 'I'm sorry . . . but
   you all looked so *lovely* . . .' and then . . .
   it all got a bit . . . whatsisname . . . Philip Larkin . . .
   we're all following the antique black and white Rolls
      Royce to
   the reception . . .
   and over the motorway . . .
   on one of those bridges . . .
   a horse and carriage with *another* bride . . .
   going *over* us . . .
   and as we're eating our salmon en croute, peas . . .
   lemon potatoes . . .
   indifferent Chablis . . .
   in The Coachman Suite . . .
   the eau de nil crew are on chicken
   à la something concealed in a creamy mushroom
      sauce in
   The Highwayman Suite . . .
   and when I pop to point Percy at
   the Porcelain . . .
   through the vestibule window . . .
   I see a horse-drawn carriage bearing
   yet another *whipped-creamed* bride
   and her *frock-coated* groom drawing
   up at the door for another
   Saturday wedding day . . .
   and all over . . .
   lots of two peoples are doing this thing
   and . . .
   they look so *young*
   and . . .

   He struggles for . . .

faces without . . .

faces clear of . . .

empty of . . .

He gets there . . .

stupid!

They all look . . . stupid . . .
their expressions   stupid
as if . . .
they have absolutely no idea at all why
they are doing what they are doing
who they are who she is who he is
what they've got on where they are
what they are promising to do
what it *means* . . . a wedding . . .

Music . . . dramatic, 'something wicked this way comes'-type soundtrack from Casablanca *plays . . .*

Evelyn
Now.

Peter
What 'Now', darling?

Evelyn (*very politely*) Who are you?

A pause. Peter ceases being so tiddly.

Peter
Peter.
Your husband.

Evelyn
Who are you?

Peter
Your husband your husband your husband.

He's very tired . . .

I think I'll go and get out of these . . .

Have a shower.

Sandwich.

Would you like a sandwich, darling?

Evelyn gets up.

No. Don't get up.

I'm having a shower first.

She continues, moving towards him.

No.
No.
I'll just be upstairs.

She gets hold of his sleeve. Holds on.

No.
No, darling . . . Evelyn . . .

He tries to disengage her from his sleeve.

Evelyn (*distressed*)
oh
oh
oh!

Peter
No!

Stay there.

Stay.
Evelyn . . .

Well come then.

Come on then.

Come.

*Evelyn stretches out her hand to him. They move
together as . . .*

TWO
THE ENGAGEMENT

*A woman, Sally, comes forward through the fog.
She smooths two dresses hanging up and tells us . . .*

Sally
A wedding story
Okay
I was at a reception . . .
naturally
Seating Plan had me
on the table where they put
all the Flotsam . . .
The Divorced, The Widowed
The Gay . . .
The Low-Marriage-Potential Crowd . . .
The Difficult-To-Slot-In-The-Big-World Brigade . . .
opposite and one across . . .
woman . . . my age . . .

Grace is seen . . .

thought she was straight on account of her shoes . . .
but
on the Flotsam Table so . . .
possibly she's . . . (*gay*)
Easy On The Eye . . .
and . . .
foreign! (*Oh, the Heaven Of It!*)
and . . .
to talk to . . . kind of . . . *larky* . . .

Lot of repressed smiling and looking . . . very strong immediate attraction. This is Romance!

Grace

. . . groom's mother's hat's *lovely*, isn't it . . .?

She's lying.

Sally

No.

Grace

Not a fan of the Sydney Opera House look?

Sally

I think it works as a public building . . .

Grace

. . . intersecting an expanse of sun-sparkling harbour water . . .

Sally

yes . . . but I don't think it works on someone with a face like
a smacked bum . . .

Grace

. . . you're saying my Auntie Lily has a face like a smacked bum?

Sally

Oh. Dear.
I'm sorry.

Grace

No. You're really not. (*Pause.*)

Sally

Blown it.

Grace

You would have to smack a bum very hard
and very long to get it quite that . . . pink

Sally

And I go . . . *that* pink!
Imagine!

Grace

Oh . . . Best Man's Speech!

Sally

Fuck!

Both listen.

Speech is very witty
Drinking references
Shagging references
Penis Penis Penis
her name's . . .

Grace

Grace.

Sally

Kind of a name's *that*?

Grace

From the Latin *gratia* apparently.
It means *grace* in the sense of the undeserved
favour of God . . .
Or the Greek *charis* . . .
to rejoice . . .

*They look at each other for a time. The Best Man's
Speech starts up again as . . .*

Sally

Marriage as . . . Prison Sentence
Marriage as . . . Institution but who wants to live in an

Institution? . . .
Husband as . . . Innocent Victim
Wife as . . . (*interestingly*) Hitler! . . .

She looks at Grace. Grace equally interested . . .

and then . . .
but seriously
Love
Connubial Bliss . . .
Commitment
Sharing
Security
Togetherness
on their long journey through Life . . .
Ladies and Gentlemen
The Bride and Groom!

Champagne corks pop . . . cheering . . .

Sally
Lot to drink
Lot (*moving . . .*)
Lot of covert, anti-wedding sniggering
Lot
with . . .

Grace
Grace . . .

Sally
and that in-class-no-laughing-at-the-back
– throwback sensation
activates my bladder into 'Go'
and I'm in the Ladies . . .
my senses are reeling . . .
The Sentries At The Door In My Heart
are temporarily Off-Watch . . .
then she comes in . . .

17

Now they are in the Ladies as . . .

Ah. Grace. Rejoice.
Would you like to come into one of these
cubicles and   explore?

Grace

Outrageous.

Sally

Well. Forward. End Cubicle.
Come in here.
With me.

Grace

You are. Outrageous.

Sally

They expect Our Table to behave badly.
That's why they invite us to weddings.

Grace

My Auntie Lily invited me because she *hoped*
I'd meet a nice man . . .

Sally

Well . . . the night is young.
Coming?

Pause.

Grace

Hope to be.

They find this very funny . . . and they . . .

Sally

And we go together into the end cubicle . . .

To us . . .

Don't kid yourself . . .
A Wedding Story.
It always starts with Sex . . .

In the cubicle . . . sexy . . . but also funny . . .

Sally
Lock the door.

Grace
That'll mean we're Engaged.

This is very funny . . . they both laugh . . .

Sally
We can't hang about
every member of The Wedding
has been drinking for England . . .
The Men are peeing in The Rose Garden . . .
I sense Sydney Opera House
about to intersect the glittering expanse
of our Harbour of Love . . .
The Ladies Powder Room at
The Saracen's Head Hotel Bickley
is Ours Alone for but a moment . . .
. . . the younger bridesmaids
are pattering this way . . .

Speed Is Of The Essence . . .

Casablanca *soundtrack music as . . .*

. . . and there's locks and cramped spaces
and sanitary engineering
and fluids and U-bends and tissues
and getting cosmically caught with
passion pants down
Oh Brief and Fleeting Love!!!!!

Sally walks off leaving . . .

Grace
    Well.
    It'll make a good story!
    'No . . . guess what *I* did once . . .!'
    'At a *Wedding*'
    'In *England*!'
    So.
    Phone Numbers. (*exchanged*)
    She dances . . .
    very badly . . .
    with an oldish man . . .
    then . . . (*gesture for 'she goes'*)

    *Sally and Peter come together . . . some appalling
    dancing . . .*

Sally
    I'll ring you!

Grace
    '*Yeah . . . Right!*'
    A Lift offer from . . . Sydney Opera House.
    Sail off.
    Sunset.

    I'll just forget *all* about her!

    Grace retires to forget all about her as . . .

THREE
TELLTALE STAINS

Peter (*matter of fact*)
    She's stopped reading novels
    your mother
    since we retired

Evelyn

I'm non-fiction.
Can't see the point of fiction.
Made-up stories.
I like facts
truth
details
Fiction!
well . . . who's got the *time*!

Peter

She wants to be with me all the time
your mother
arrange my day around her
sweet
bit of a second honeymoon actually . . .

Sally

'Sassy OAPs Enjoy Twilight Sex
Roguish Father Tells Queasy Daughter.'

Peter smiles at Sally. She smiles back . . .

Not a badtempered woman . . .
never a swearer . . .
fucking hell no . . .

Evelyn tuts slightly . . .

but . . .
started to become much more
abrupt

short fuse

fierce

and

these

small inexplicable moments of confusion . . .

Evelyn (*furious*)

    . . . I was there *fifteen* minutes early and
    Miss Busy-Reading-My-Hello-Magazine
    at Reception says 'Yes?'
    and I say 'Mrs Swan. Cut and Blow Dry at eleven-
      thirty'
    and she says 'We haven't got you down!' I said
    'Tuesday the sixth at eleven-thirty . . .
    I made the appointment last time I was here.
    You wrote it down'
    She says 'We've no record of it . . . '

Sally

    She's in 'A Cut Above' on Victoria Road,
    while in 'Hair Today!' on Halifax Avenue
    where she *has* made the appointment
    Shaznay trainee
    and Dale   stylist
    wait in vain . . .
    and driving with Evelyn
    just as   hairy

Peter

    Darling, what are you doing?

Evelyn (*furious*) . . .

    I'm just filling her with petrol and
    that . . . *man* . . . in the blue . . . *car* . . . just . . . calm as you
    like starts helping himself to the fuel thing *right* next
    door to me!
    The bloody *cheek*!
    The bloody damn *cheek* of it!
    I *slapped* his (*action for 'face'*) for him!!!!!
    The *bloody cheek*!

    She sits down . . .

Sally
>and then . . .
>and then one day . . .
>one *golden* evening . . .

Evelyn (*with great delight and warmth* . . .)
>Dolly and Jack
>*Tuxford* came for dinner!
>I haven't seen her since they lived in Mottisham
>and she's lost a *lot* of weight
>it's taken ten years off her!
>Wearing a *lovely* silk-knit top in a . . . you know the
>inside of an *oyster shell* . . .?

Peter
>*He's* still the same boring old gasbag . . .
>now doing an Open University on . . .

Evelyn/Peter
>Societal Constructs in Early Saxon Settlements . . .

Evelyn
>We start with my butternut squash and cinnamon
>>soup . . .

Peter
>. . . served with the rest of the champagne . . .
>the Veuve Cliquot . . . well, we hadn't seen them for
>>*years*!

>*They continue with parallel marital speaking . . .*

Evelyn
>and then I'd just done lamb . . . because they're
>both quite *careful* eaters . . . but with some borlotti beans
>in a tomato garlicky sauce as well as vegetables . . . /
>broccoli . . . leeks
>roast potatoes   for the men

Peter *(speaking over from . . . /)*
 I'd got a very nice red from
 my Wine Club . . . it was a Grand Cru . . . grenache
   grape . . .
 very nice . . .

Evelyn
 and a raspberry pavlova . . .

Peter
 . . . very good Montrachet . . . and all the *chat* . . .

Evelyn
 No, no no, Jack! . . .
 Early Saxon Societal Attitudes *research* is *just* the *same*
 as . . .

 She is always trying to stop Jack jumping in . . .

 being a doctor is . . . detective work . . .
 it's cause and effect . . . for example . . .
 a therosclerotic obstruction in the artery that nourishes
 a segment of heart muscle will cause infarction . . .
 a tumor that produces an over-supply of insulin
 drastically reduces levels of glucose in the blood
 preventing proper brain nutrition and leading to
   coma . . .

Peter
 . . . shall I carve you a bit more lamb, Jack . . .?

Evelyn
 a loop of gut becomes twisted around a strand of
 internal post-operative scar tissue . . . and the consequent
 intestinal obstruction produces distension, vomiting,
 dehydration . . .

Peter
 Dolly . . . bit more wine in your glass, my dear . . .?

Evelyn

and chemical imbalances in the blood
which can lead to arrythmia . . .
cause and effect
cause and effect . . .
the patient comes to the doctor with one or more
clues . . . and the detective work begins . . .

Peter

Darling, your sleeve is in your borlotti beans . . .

Evelyn lifts her wrist impatiently as . . .

Evelyn

. . . it is to the series of events that has led to the
observable set of symptoms and other clinical findings
that we refer to when we use the term . . .
pathophysiology . . .

Peter

Darling . . . you're *lecturing* . . .

Evelyn

. . . Anything to stop Jack banging on about Saxon
Settlements!
ay, Dolly? . . . Dolly . . . have some more broccoli . . .
Jack . . . 'physiologia'
from the Greek root . . . 'an inquiry into the nature
of things'
and 'pathos' . . . 'suffering' . . . put them together and
we have the
essence of the doctor's quest . . . which is to make
inquiry into
the nature of suffering . . . so it becomes the doctor's
job to
identify the instigating cause of sickness by tracing
back along
the sequence until he has found the ultimate culprit . . .

Peter

Darling, you're *still* lecturing . . .

Evelyn

Well, I'm *tiddly* darling . . . I *always* lecture when I'm tiddly . . .

microbial or hormonal, chemical or mechanical, genetic or

environmental, malignant or benign, congenital or newly-acquired . . .

let me have my say, Jack . . . we've been in Anglo-Saxon Kent

for long enough this evening! . . . the investigation is done to

the body by the perpetrator. The crime is reconstructed

and a treatment instigated that rids the patient of the instigator

of the disease . . . Peter! . . . Dolly's glass is *completely* empty! . . . in a

sense, every doctor is a pathopsychologist . . . the aim is to excise

the pathology . . . destroy it with drugs or X-ray . . . counteract it with

antidotes, strengthen the organs it is attacking . . . kill its causative

germs . . . or simply hold it in check until the body's own defences

can overwhelm it . . . a plan of action must be organised against

each disease if the patient is to stand any chance of overcoming it . . .

Peter

Evelyn . . . I'm going to hit you with the leg of lamb if you don't . . .

During the next speech, Evelyn gets the hiccups . . .

Evelyn
. . . when a physician engages in combat to struggle
against his patient's mortality . . . (*hic*) his knowledge
of cause and effect is the armoury to which he turns
to help him (*hic*) choose his weapons . . . Dolly . . . (*hic*)
have some cream on that . . .
Pavlova . . .
(*hic*) Peter . . .
(*hic*) can you get me a glass of (*hic*) water . . .?

Sally
Every, every illness . . .
we can fight . . .

*Evelyn drinks from the glass of water . . . cured of
hiccups as . . .*

her educated mind tells her
and she tells us

Peter
Can't get a word in *edgeways*!

Sally
Next morning . . .

Swirls of fog . . . dramatic Casablanca *music . . .*

Evelyn
What?

Who?

No.

Sally
Evelyn
can't remember any of it.

Peter
Jack!
Dolly!

Raspberry Pavlova!
Saxon Societal Constructs!
The Evelyn Swan Commemorative Lecture on
Pathophysiology!
The Hiccups!

Evelyn is completely mystified . . . disbelieving . . .

Sally
No amount of explanation can convince her
that Dolly and Jack had been there . . .

Evelyn
No.   No.   No.

Peter
Look!
Four best dinner plates! . . . *four* red, *four* white wine
    glasses!
Four *flutes*!
For the champagne! £23.99 a bottle!
Look . . . bottom shelf of the fridge . . .
Remains of a *Leg of Lamb*!

Evelyn
I've no memory of it.
None.

*A pause. She looks at him. He looks away. Some mist
swirls. Then . . .*

Peter
Well. Sometimes I forget things too.
The champagne. Wine.
The excitement.
Maybe later.
She'll remember.
Maybe later.

Sally
Frightened Old Fucker.

*She strokes her father's hair absent-mindedly, making
the parting sharp . . . She roots around in her
pocket/bag for a comb . . .*

he almost convinces himself
that the whole thing
is
insignificant
as . . .

Finds instead . . .

FOUR
THE HONEYMOON

A piece of paper . . .

Sally
Her phone number
written on a piece torn off the
wedding breakfast menu . . .
I *really* wasn't . . .
it was just going to be one of those things . . .
(*Sings.*) 'just one of those crazy things . . .
a trip-to-the-moon-on-gossamer-wings . . .'
but my hands
quite independent of my brain
picked up the phone
dialled her number
and . . .
my body . . .
quite without permission from my intellect . . .
went off for a red-wine-intensive supper with her . . .

She is with Grace. It is the end of a long evening . . .
Sally is coming back from Grace's bathroom . . .

(*still to us*) that's Lust . . . isn't it?
I mean . . . that's not Love!

Grace
Okay?

Sally
Yes. Nice bathroom.

Grace
Well, it's not The Saracen's Head Bickley . . . but . . .

Sally
But then . . . where is?

They look at each other. Then . . .

Grace
Now.
Er.
Okay.
Look.
What happens now?
How do we go on with it? I mean . . . do we
go on with it . . . or was it just a fuck in a toilet
at a wedding? . . . because of course if we end
here that's fine it'll make a great competitive
bid in 'where's the wierdest place you've ever
fucked' conversations . . . I mean . . . (*furious*) I'm
always the first to do this! . . .
look . . . I'm feeling
great *waves* of affection for you . . . and with
just a bit more I don't know . . . *reciprocity* from
you the waves of affection could become . . .

Sally
Reciprocity?

30

Grace

Isn't that a Word? . . . where you say back to me
'Yes . . . *I'm* feeling great waves of affection for *you* . . .'

Sally

Ripples . . . I've got ripples . . .

Grace

How you are in the first three weeks
is how you'll be for the rest of the relationship . . .
I'm feeling waves you're feeling ripples . . .
It's doomed.

Evelyn (*to us*)

Has someone been in this cupboard?
Everything's been moved round!

Sally

Grace . . .

Grace

Yes

Sally

You say 'Come into my bedroom and see
if we can capture the majesty and grandeur
of that first time in the Saracen's Head Hotel Bickley
Ladies Powder Room cubicle . . . '

Grace (*in French*)

Come into my bedroom and see if we
can capture / the majesty and grandeur of
that first time in the Saracen's Head Hotel Bickley
Ladies Powder Room cubicle . . .

Sally (*as Grace repeats . . . /*)

I haven't got time for this!
I haven't got the energy!
I know this . . . this is the *honeymoon*!
This is the easy bit!

the being in bed in the daytime bit . . .
the Swooning ! . . .

Peter

You see . . . (*lecturing*)
the *Medieval* concept of Love . . .

Thus possed to and fro
Al stereless within a boot am I
Amydde the see, betwixen wyndes two,
Thet in contrarie stonden evere mo,
Allas, what is this wondre maladie?
For hote of cold, for cold of hote, I die.

from Chaucer . . . look at *The Knight's Tale* . . .
Petrarch, Dante . . . through Wyatt . . . Spenser . . .
even, I *suppose*, Shakespeare . . .
Rosalind . . . *As You Like It* . . . says
'Love is merely a madness, and I tell you,
deserves as well a dark house and a whip
as madmen do; and the reason why they are
not so punished and cured is that the lunacy
is so ordinary that the whippers are in love too . . .'
. . . was that it was *an illness*!
that you *caught*

Sally

Yes, Dad.

Peter

You became *not* yourself . . .

Sally

Dad!

Grace

That man . . . at the wedding . . .
who you danced rock'n'roll with?
Was that your father?

32

Sally is embarassed . . .

Sally
That was my father, yes. But that
wasn't me.

Evelyn (*to us*)
Somebody's been wearing my shoes!

Grace
Your mother   is she . . .
around . . .?

FIVE
AN IMMACULATE WAISTBAND

. . . which is a familiar family recounting of . . .

Sally
Peter Swan
met Evelyn Phyllis Roderick
when she was
nineteen and he was twenty-one . . .

She cues her mother in . . .

'I was wearing . . . '

Evelyn
. . . I was wearing a navy blue crepe dress

*Evelyn is fully compos-mentis. It is some time earlier.
Sally mimics her mother's precise hand movements
with affectionate scorn as . . .*

with pin tucks under the bust . . .
and a skirt cut on the bias so it . . .

Sally/Evelyn
swirled in a *perfect* circle when I danced . . .

*Evelyn dances. Sally joins her. Evelyn is a very good
dancer . . . Peter watches . . .*

Peter
She looked lovely. She looked lovely!

Evelyn breaks off dancing as . . .

Evelyn
. . . and he was in a corduroy suit!
I'd never seen a corduroy *suit* before!

Sally
What were the trousers like, Mum?

*Both women continue their delicate hand movements
as . . .*

Evelyn
Beautifully cut.
Plenty of material falling with pleats
from an *immaculate* waistband . . .

*Sally continues the precise hand movements over the
next speech, which makes Evelyn smile . . .*

Sally
. . . so you couldn't see how *packed* his
lunchbox was . . . you could only speculate
as to the size and *magnificence* of his fishing tackle
    . . you
couldn't get your loop out and study the
treasure trove that was his family jewels . . .

*Evelyn slaps Sally playfully hard on wrist. A mother's
slap.*

Evelyn
Oh, you didn't know anything about that side of things /

Peter
/ you *tried*. Got you nowhere.

Evelyn
  till you were married . . .

Sally
  . . . which they duly were at . . .

Sally/Evelyn
  St Christopher's church, Peel Lane, Ottisford . . .
  fourteenth of May . . .
  a *lovely* day for it . . .

Evelyn
  . . . my dress was a heavy shantung silk . . . floor-length
  with a demi-monde train . . . edged at the bodice, cuffs
  and hem with *tiny* tear-drop ersatz pearls . . .

  Sally is mouthing and miming occasionally . . .
  fondly . . . laconically . . .

Peter
  . . . I turned to see her come down the aisle . . .
  and . . . my eyes filled with tears, Sally . . .
  I had to turn and look up at the *ceiling* . . .
  make the tears drop back in . . .

  To blink them back . . .

Evelyn
  . . . we had the reception at The Bunch Of Grapes,
  Mottingham . . . and everybody was lovely apart
  from that doctor friend of your cousin Anne's . . .
  with the black tongue from all that red wine
  and the food stains all over her blouse
  and the *language* . . .
  what was she called?

Peter
  Ivy Vickerman?

Evelyn (*absolute contempt for this suggestion*)
  No!

No!
No!!!!

A long pause . . .

*Evelyn realises she must be very clear in dealing with
these very stupid people . . .*

Evelyn
. . . the one in the grey pinstripe costume . . .
with the fox-fur . . . and cloche hat . . . *black* cloche
hat! . . .

To Sally . . .

she was sitting next to *you* . . . right next to *you* . . .
what was she called? . . .

A pause . . .

Sally
I don't know, Mum.
I wasn't there.

Evelyn (*to Peter . . . huge, revolted vehemence*)
That's right!
Get your *fucking cunting girlfriend* to come and *lie*
to me!

Sally
Dad . . .

Peter
No.

No!!!!!!

Sally picks up a dress on a hanger. Shows it to Evelyn.

Sally
What d'you think of this, Mum?

Evelyn approves and recognises . . .

Evelyn
Oh!
That's *kingfisher* blue, isn't it?

Sally/Evelyn
It's blue with green sort of *underneath* . . .

SIX
AND THEN THERE'S COURTING . . .

Sally (*to us*)
. . . And then
there's *courting* . . .
giving your presents . . .

Grace comes to her, incredulously holding . . .

Grace
A whoopee cushion?

Sally
A Design Comedy Classic . . .
I was in a shop by The British Museum and . . .

She mimes seeing it by surprise . . .

you have to blow air into it . . .
like this . . .

she kisses Grace deeply on the lips . . .

Grace (*singing*)
'. . . take my breath away . . .'

(*and*) '. . . up, up and away . . .
in my beautiful balloon . . .'

As Grace blows air into it . . .

Sally
The bits of you you take and give to them
you're so *generous* when
you're courting . . .
'here's my *best* bits . . .
I'm *Adorable*'
okay, now you put it on a chair
and somebody sits down on it . . .

as Grace puts the whoopee cushion on the chair . . .
then walks away . . . walks back as . . .

and . . .
you're on your absolutely *best* behaviour . . .
because you want this person who you
like to like you even *more* . . .
so the romance the fever the illness
the madness continues to
invade your senses . . .

Grace sits down on the whoopee cushion . . .

Sally
What d'you think?

Grace
It's *so* romantic.

Sally
You can make it do different ones . . .
depending on the pressure you . . .

Grace (*as Sally blows it up again*)
. . . so
it's not just the one magical experience then . . .?

Sally
Oh no.
It's like multiple orgasms . . .

(to us) and Courting's when you get to tell all your
stories . . .

*To Grace, as Grace experiments with the different
sounds you can get out of a whoopee cushion . . .*

Sally
I got one in my stocking one Christmas . . .
and Mum and Dad were *Princely* about
the number of times
one would sit on it . . .
and . . .

Whoopee cushion farts . . .

Evelyn
Peter . . . was that rude noise *you?*

Sally
and then I'd put it on *her* chair
and he'd be like . . .

Whoopee cushion farts . . .

Peter
Evelyn!
Did you have too many baked beans
yesterday?

Sally laughing . . .

Sally
And they were *Stars*
totally surprised
every time
all Christmas Day
then
Boxing Day morning
I put it on Mum's chair
and it's . . .

Farting noise again . . .

Evelyn
Alright, I think we've had quite enough of that, Sally!

Sally pauses, five-year-old face, body, invades her . . .

Sally
Fucker.
Fucking Tricky Fucker!
Gives . . . then . . . *Takes* it Away!

Grace
Have you told her about me?

Sally
well . . .   no.
(*to us*) Why should I?
Not going to be permanent, this.
This is just a . . . diversion . . .
Well . . . live in the moment, right?
and anyway . . .

SEVEN
IN SICKNESS AND IN HEALTH

Peter picks up a golf trophy . . . is dusting it as Evelyn comes in . . .

Evelyn
What are doing?

Peter
Dusting, darling.

Danger-approaching music plays. Evelyn very paranoid . . . therefore very dangerous suddenly . . .

Evelyn
What are you doing in my house?
What are you doing with my husband's things?

Peter

It's my golf trophy. Look.
Peter Swan. Hazel Dene Golf Clu . . .

Evelyn

Those are my husband's golf trophies.

She goes to him, wrestles the trophy from his hands . . .

Evelyn

Give that to me!
Steal from my house!!!

She starts to break things, throw things at him . . .

I'm calling my daughter!
Tell her what you're doing!

She dials.

Sally!
There's a man here stealing Daddy's things!

Sally

Where's Daddy, Mum?

Evelyn

I don't know!
There's just this man!

Sally

Put him on, Mum.
Put that man on, Mum.
I'll talk to him.

Evelyn

My daughter wants a word with you!

Peter

Sally . . .

Sally

Dad.

Pause. An awful moment.

What's she doing?

Peter
She's . . .

Peter is savagely attacked by Evelyn. He is still. Sally listens.

Evelyn (*same time as . . .*)
Thief! Robber! Steal . . .?
Steal? Steal? Doesn't belong to you!
That's my husband's!

Peter (*same time as Evelyn*)
Evelyn . . .
Evelyn . . . it's me . . . it's Peter . . . Peter . . .
Evelyn . . .

Sally
Dad.
Get out of there.
Leave the house right away.
I'm calling the police . . .

Peter
Police came. Patrol car!
Right smack front of the house . . .! (*the disgrace*)

Evelyn
He's not my husband.
Come with me.
I'll show you a picture of my husband!

Photo still of Peter and Evelyn's wedding . . .

Peter
The policeman's *Jack* from The Golf Club!
Five handicap.
says . . .

42

'This man looks like your husband,
standing right here . . .'

Evelyn
He's *not* my husband!

Peter
Denise came in from next door . . .

Evelyn
Denise . . .!

Peter
Denise said 'Evelyn, you know I love you
and I wouldn't lie to you.
This man is Peter . . .
turn around and look.'
and she did just as she was told . . .

Evelyn turns round. Sees Peter . . . as if for the first time . . .

Evelyn
Peter!
Oh, thank God you're here!
Somebody's been in here trying to
steal your golf trophies!!!!

Sally
Fucking Drama Queen.

Evelyn
Sally!

Sally
I'm living about two hundred miles away
but . . .

She goes towards Evelyn, who . . .

... greets Sally with great love. Sally sits Evelyn down with her ...

Sally
What's Alzheimer's Disease, Mum?

Evelyn
Well, love ... The fundamental pathology of
Alzheimer's Disease
is the progressive degeneration and loss
of vast numbers of nerve cells in those portions
of the brain's cortex that are associated with
the so-called higher functions,
such as
memory
learning
judgement.

Looks to see if Sally is taking it in ...

Sally
Mmm.   Fuck.

Evelyn slaps Sally lightly for swearing.

memory
learning
judgement

Evelyn looks at Sally's hair in a 'it-won't-do' motherly way ... as ...

Evelyn
The severity and nature of the patient's dementia
at any given time are proportional to the number and
location of cells that have been affected.

She starts tidying Sally's hair as . . .

Evelyn
The decrease in nerve-cell population is in itself
sufficient to explain the memory loss and other
cognitive disabilities, but there is another factor
that seems to play a role as well . . .
this needs a good haircut . . .
a marked decrease in acetylcholine . . .
the chemical used by these cells
to transmit messages . . .
am I lecturing, darling?

Sally
Oh yes.

Sally takes Evelyn's hand in hers . . .

(*to us*) Here's the dreadful irony . . .
Evelyn is a doctor . . .
was a doctor . . .?

Evelyn
these are the basic elements of what we know
about Alzheimer's . . .

She turns over Sally's hands . . .

you need to spend some time on your nails, lady . . .

The long lists of cause, effects, treatments
in other illnesses
have no analogy to the present state of
our knowledge . . .
or ignorance . . .
of Alzheimer's.
We know not a whit more
about what might cure it
than we do about what might cause it.

Evelyn

I've got it   haven't I?

Sally

Yes, Mum.

Evelyn

Oh Sally.

She sees she has Sally's hand in hers. She grips it tightly. Fog plays around their feet as . . .

With the kingfisher blue . . .
My *dark* navy court shoes.
Not the black.
Not the black!

NINE
THE MIDDLE OF THE NIGHT

Sally

And
in the middle of the night . . .

Darkness on all but Sally's face . . . we hear . . .

Peter

What?

Evelyn

What are you doing here?
Since when?
Since when?
Since When?????
Does a brother sleep with his sister?
You're disgusting!
Get out of here!
Out!
Out, you incestuous bastard!

46

Light widens to reveal Peter standing at the edge of Sally's space . . .

Sally
How long has this been going on?

Peter
It's not all the time.
I come down and sleep on the . . .

Sofa bed, where Sally is . . . both listen as . . .

Evelyn (*absolute hate*)
I won't have it
I won't have it
I will not have it!
(*to us*) Who do they think they *are*????
the thing is
I feel just . . .

She can't find the word 'fine' . . . only the smile and the body attitude . . .

look at me
we do walks every weekend
I'm more (*fit*) than most of the
younger women in . . .

She can't find the word for Aerobics Class . . . acts it . . .

up down . . . what you
wear . . . (*leotard . . .*)
Peter and I   we still
its not *exciting* any more
it's *comfortable*   but
we still   most weeks
manage   a bit of a
quite *athletic* . . .

Can't find . . . 'cuddle' . . . 'sex' . . .

47

with . . . *willy!* . . . that thing . . .

I've looked after myself!

It

Oh dear

you lose . . .

I don't want strangers wiping my . . . (*what?*)

I think if I talk to Fitzpatrick . . .
get him to give me a diet sheet
keep exercising my . . .

Can't find . . . 'mind', acts it . . .

keep . . .
we'll be . . .

you see
Peter's not much of a . . .
it's not his strength . . .
and (*points to Sally . . . what is her name?*)
well . . . she's got her own life to . . .
and . . . (*can't remember*) . . . *someone* . . .

She looks to where . . .

TEN
SOMEONE

Somewhere in the fog, Robin appears.

Robin (*as Bogart*)
    'Of all the
    gin joints in all the towns
    in all the world . . .
    she comes into my gin joint . . .'

48

Evelyn (*utter joy*)
Oh!

Robin performs excellent impersonation of Dooley Wilson . . . Evelyn as Ingrid.

Ingrid
Hullo Sam . . .

Dooley
Hullo Miss Elsa.
I never expect to see you again.

Ingrid
Yes, it's been a long time.

Dooley
Yes Ma'am, a lot of water under the bridge.

Ingrid
Some of the old songs, Sam

Dooley
Yes Ma'am.

Piano music from Casablanca *plays under . . .*

Evelyn (*enchanted*)
Yes!

Robin as . . .

Ingrid
Play it once, Sam. For old time's sake.

Dooley
I don't know what you mean, Miss Elsa.

Ingrid (*whisper*)
Play it Sam. Play 'As Time Goes By'.

Dooley
Oh, I cain't remember it, Miss Elsa . . .
I'm a li'l rusty on it . . .

Evelyn laughs, claps as . . .

Ingrid
I'll hum it for you . . .
da day day day day da
da day day day day day da . . .

Evelyn is in Heaven as . . .

Dooley
You must remember this . . .

Sally sings it quietly as . . .

Bogart
I thought I told you never to play
that song again, Sam . . .

*The soundtrack score after Bogart's interruption plays
as . . .*

Evelyn
More!

Fog envelops him as Evelyn, we see, is crying . . .

Who are you?
Who are you?

I'll talk to Fitzpatrick about care
. . . where we stand financially . . .
I've sent patients to council places that are
perfectly . . .

She thinks . . .

perfectly . . .

Laughs ruefully . . .

rows of *frightful* chairfuls of old . . .

Can't find 'women'.

that'll teach you . . .
Do As You Would Be Done By . . .

Can't remember her name . . .

Now . . .
Who are you . . .? (*no idea*)

I'll be alright
I'll be alright
It'll all be alright! (*She's convinced.*)

Peter?
Peter?

She keeps calling his name over . . . as . . .

Sally (*to Peter*)
She can't stay with you.
We have to find somewhere for her.
Somewhere *safe*.
Don't we?
Don't we?

ELEVEN
IN SICKNESS AND IN HEALTH . . .

Sally
Well . . . this is where he should say . . .

Peter
I can look after her.
I'd like to do that.
Look after her.
It'll be alright.

Sally
Well . . .
He married her . . .

He promised to love honour and all that
until Death Do Them Part!
It's Down To Him!
But he doesn't.
He just says . . .

Peter

I'm tired.

Find somewhere for her.

Just for . . .

Peter

Yes.

Sally

Of course, this is the moment
I should step in . . .
say
'*I'm* not married.
I've no family of my own . . .
I'll take care of her . . .'
But I don't . . . it's not how we do it these days . . .

Peter

I still love your mother.
But . . .

He bursts into tears . . .

Sally

Well, I'm not having this!
No!
What happened to Courtly Love, Professor Swan?
Parfit gentil fucking knight, dad!
This isn't in my contract.
I'm *The Daughter*!
I'm *The One Who Gets Looked After*!
I'm *The One Who GETS AWAY WITH MURDER*!

52

She's The *Parent*!
He's The Parent!
Children looking after Parents!
When did *that* start?
I've had no choice in all this . . .
I'm getting on with my own life!
I've constructed a whole network of intricate
dysfunctional relationships of my own to
mismanage I can't drop all that and buy into this
fucking . . . *Chechnia*!
fucking . . . *Kosovo*!
fucking . . . *Holocaust*!
I haven't . . . *Time* . . . for this because . . .
to get back to *my* life . . .
because . . .
a fucking *flanker* attack!

TWELVE
THE PROPOSAL

She walks into the end of a long discussion about 'where is our relationship going . . . ?'

Grace

I want to be married.
I want to be married. To you.

Sally

Agghh. Grace! Grace!
Why? Why? Why?

Grace

I love you. I want to be with you forever.

Sally

Agh! Don't hold back. Say what you mean . . .

Grace
   And I want a public acknowledgement of it
   . . . Like everybody else.

Sally
   Oh please God . . . not *politics* . . .

Grace
   It's a simple human right . . .

Sally
   Getting a bit edgy getting a bit queasy all getting
   a bit Marge Piercy a bit early Feminism and
   late religious and *awful* marriage of concepts
   I mean
   It's not as if we'll have children . . . (*big mistake* . . .)

Grace
   We might.
   We might.
   It's the year 2000. It's possible. People do it.
   Why not?

   A phone rings . . . lights up gradually on . . . Robin . . .

Sally (*phone to Robin . . .*)
   It's like one of those dodgy fucking
   low-budget independent lesbian films . . .
   She said 'Let's get married'

Robin (*mock-serious voice*)
   '. . . well,
   technically, that's not possible in the United Kingdom . . . '

Sally
   She'll get some fucking *Dane* shipped over.
   Or we'll have to go to fucking *Amsterdam*!
   She said 'Let's have children'

Robin (*ditto*)
   . . . 'Well, biologically, that's not possible'

Sally
The fucking Turkey Baster Road . . .

Robin (*queasy*)
Feeling a bit faint now . . .

Sally
I became a lesbian to get out of all that . . .

Robin (*ditto*)
'Well, our research intimates that
you became a lesbian because of a homosexual
gene which means it is neither *your* fault nor
the fault of your tragically-disappointed parents . . .'

Sally
How's the weather in Berkeley?

Robin
In the seventies . . .

Sally
Fuck you.

Robin
I'm missing seasons.
Fuck you.

How's Evelyn . . .?

*Sally is back with Grace. The lighting is all bars . . .
impressionistic prison as . . .*

Sally (*to Grace . . .*)
. . . I can't do this now.
Shall we not talk about it tonight?
Can we wait? . . . seem to be in waiting mode just at
the moment . . .?
I don't know if I can ever do it.
I feel sick.
The whole idea makes me queasy.

It's a health thing.
I need to look after myself.
Be unfaithful a lot.
Carry a big inhalant of . . . freedom. Just In Case.
Is it stuffy in here?
Place is full of smoke!
No air.

. . . Can we open the window?

Escape.

A plane flies over . . .

THIRTEEN
AN AIRPORT HEAD

Robin, waiting at an airport . . .

Robin
Need something to read on the plane . . .
being my mother's son . . .
do the research
know what you're talking about
(*quoting*) 'facts
truth
details . . .
I mean . . . *Fiction?*
well, who's got time?'
I go for factual . . .
(*reads*) . . . 'the single most important one is
a stark statistic . . . Alzheimer's disease strikes more
than 11 per cent of the population over sixty-five . . .
by the year 2030, the population over sixty-five
will reach 60 million or more . . .
the magnitude of the problem is staggering . . .'

Takes it in and . . .

And . . .

alchemises it . . .

a great premise for a *film* scenario . . .
It's 2030. The Near Future.
The Young . . . among them . . . DiCaprio . . .
live in digitally-created fortress cities.
Outside the walls . . . in the wild country . . .
The Old . . . The Dangerously Forgetful . . .
played by a host of veteran actors . . . Dames of
The British Theatre . . . Maggie Smith . . . Diana Rigg . . .
plucky little Thora Hurd . . . roam about . . .
helped and fed only by a small band of
caring Robin Hood types . . .
led by a tough, sassy, leather-clad . . . Julia Roberts.
She breaks into DiCaprio's electronically-surveillance-
protected apartment to steal food and supplies . . .
Maggie, Diana and Thora are in the forest,
scene-grabbingly warming their gnarled hands
at a glowing fire . . .
DiCaprio catches Julie . . . her hands in the ice-box . . .
and his cold, Look-Out-For-Number-One
philosophy is challenged when, having fallen in love
with her . . . life-brightening laugh and tough honesty . . .
he defends her against a pack of rabid OAPs.
She's a Star, but she's also A Woman
and finally, she's no match on her own against The Old.
It's a love story that plugs into the Zeitgeist.

Awful reality swirls around him as . . .

(*He returns to reading . . .*) 'typically . . .
the disease is slowly
but relentlessly progressive . . .
it usually leads to death in about seven to ten years . . .
but it can progress more quickly . . .
say three to four years . . .

or
it can take as long as fifteen . . .'

He stares out of the window. The plane continues to fly as . . .

Well shit

(*as Bogart*) 'but what happens to us three
small people
don't amount to a hill of beans
in this
crazy world . . .'

He watches the crazy world below him as . . . music . . . perky version, with table-banging of 'Knock On Wood' from Casablanca *as . . .*

FOURTEEN
THE HIT

Peter is trying to do a crossword. He is exhausted. Evelyn is wondering/wandering about . . . he has to watch her as she wanders . . . in case she encounters danger to herself . . . or to others. Music underplays, irritatingly cheery . . .

Evelyn
    Ah!

Peter
    I'm tired.
    Don't do that.
    Don't do that . . . you'll . . .

    Oh, God . . . *See?*

He brings her back to him. She stands. He sits.

Just five minutes . . .
Five minutes while I do my crossword . . .
Try.
Twenty-three across. 'Variegated pepper used to get rid of rats'. Five–four.
I think it might be an anagram of . . .
no
no
no!
you watch . . .
watch then . . .

Evelyn
Oh.

She wanders off again . . .

Peter
You play with . . .
you just sit and . . . just for a *minute* . . .

She wanders. He fetches her back.

one minute

She wanders off again.

Evelyn
Ah!

Peter
No

Peter goes to Evelyn, stands quivering for a minute then he punches her hard . . . She looks at him . . . looks at her arm . . . slowly puts a hand to where she was hit. Her face is surly . . . she cowers minutely, like a dog that has been beaten . . .

FIFTEEN
HOME

Robin comes in . . . Duty Free bag. Flight bag. Books.

Robin

Home.

INTERIOR. DAY.
We are in an institutional building
It's unbearably grim.
In long shot . . .
we see an expensively-dressed man
Hugo Boss suit.   (*No we don't.*)
Louis Vuitton luggage. (*No we don't.*)
Character notes . . . successful, highly intelligent . . .
but with a slightly dangerous *edge*.
Standing end of long long corridor.
Lighting is expressionistic.
Max Reinhardt.
Close-up on his face.
Bars effect.
Face is haunted.
Bleak.
Semiotic suggestion of . . . Prison.

He looks around . . .

For £650 a week.
Very clean . . . but . . .
Christ! . . .
voice-over reveals what he is thinking.
jackbooted prison guard frogmarches past.
protagonist speaks.

To someone . . . a nice nurse . . .

Doctor Swan?
Mrs Swan?
Evelyn Phyllis Swa . . .
Evelyn . . .

Listens with polite attention as he is told . . .

you're known by your *first* name here . . .
it's friendly . . . you see . . .

large notice board says
'Today is Wednesday. The weather is sunny'

Listens with polite attention as he is told . . .

It's our Orientation Chart.
It *Helps*.

Walks into . . .

Hello, Mum.

Evelyn looks his way.

It's me.

Robin!

Evelyn's face breaks into a huge welcoming smile.

Mum . . .

Evelyn
    I love you!
    You're so handsome!
    I love you!

*She puts her arms round him and they hug and kiss
ecstatically, both crying . . .*

Robin
    I feel so *loved*!

Evelyn intensely loving . . .

Evelyn
> Darling!
> Darling!
>
> I love you!

Robin
> I love you too.
>
> Crosscut to door.
> A nurse.
> Protagonist expects Mother to
> proudly introduce prodigal son
> but . . .
>
> *Seeing nurse . . .*

Evelyn
> I love you!
> You're so beautiful.
> And I love you!

Robin
> The nurse is as loved.
>
> *He leaves as . . . Evelyn continues to say . . .*

Evelyn
> I love you!
> You're beautiful.
> I love you!
> Darling!

Sally
> And Peggy the Cleaner and Ollie the Cleaner
> and the Egg Lady
> and Ronnie the Health Visitor
> The man from Granada who is mending the
> new ward TV
> She's suddenly Dazzlingly Unfaithful
> Love The One You're With!

Forget Courtly Love, Dad.
We've accelerated into The Sixties!
Everything is a First Date!
Once
she even says it to me!

Robin into . . .

Robin
Dad!

Robin and Peter hug and shake hands, manly . . .

Just been to see her . . .

Peter puts his hand on Robin's arm . . . distressed . . .

Peter
I went and dragged her back . . .
and I rammed her back in her seat . . .
and . . .
when I sat down . . .
with my onside hand . . .
my secret   concealed   hand

I
punched her

He demonstrates to Robin . . .

right in her side
on purpose

Robin
Dad.

Peter
on *purpose*

I wanted to   really   *hurt* her

He cries.

63

Robin
She hit you once . . .
I saw her . . . when you were dancing
in the garden with Mrs Hall . . .

Peter (*still crying*)
. . . but I *deserved* that . . .!

Robin
Dad
people *hit*.
It's not the end of the world.

Peter
I'm at the end of my tether, son.

SIXTEEN
SIBLINGS

Sally arrives to Robin . . .

Sally
Okay.
Enough.
I'd like my mum back now.

Robin
Yeah.
The real one.
This 'Invasion Of The Bodysnatchers' thing.
Not working for me.

Sally
The real one. With all her loveable faults.

Robin
Even with *all* her loveable faults?

Sally (*pause*)
  Yes.

Robin
  Okay. Plus the *real* Dad.

Sally
  Not that decrepit old imposter

Peter
  I heard that!

Robin
  I'm not grown-up enough for this.
  I look sophisticated and handsome but actually I'm
    only *six*.

Sally
  Me too.
  I've got my hanky tucked in my knickers.

Robin
  And my mittens on elastic through the sleeves of my
    coat.

Sally
  I'm actually not old enough to do my own coat buttons
    up.

Robin
  And somebody's still got to cut up my food.

Sally
  We weren't told.

Robin
  It's an outrage expecting two *tiny children* like us to
    cope with this!

Sally
  It's abuse.

Robin
Yes.
Ring a Child Help Hotline.

A pause.

Sally
Give me a big American kind of hug.

Robin (*doing so*)
. . . actually . . . *you're* the oldest . . . you
should . . .

Sally
No . . . *I* boss . . . *you* do what I say. Our kid.

Robin
And I *am* the man.

Sally
True.

They hold one another tight . . .

You do everything. Sort it out. Cope.

Robin
Okay.

Pause.

Well, fuck, what can we do?

Casablanca music . . .

Robin/Sally (*dramatic voice-over voice*)
but wait
and wait

and wait . . .

Peter is sitting . . .

Peter (*to Robin*)
It's a good idea to sit out
occasionally . . . with all the others . . .
wives   husbands

children come when they can, obviously . . .

it's the family comes mainly

. . . quite useful . . . informative to swap stories . . .
exchange strategies and just talk to someone who . .
   (*understands*)

it's a good idea to bring a book because . . .
   (*it's so boring*)

nothing too *heavy* because . . .
ambience not really conducive to . . .
any sort of organised *thinking* . . .

nothing much to say really
sometimes we all just sit and cry . . .
worse than . . . Rolf Harris . . . Animal Hospital . . .
what a business . . .

*Sally sits down too. Robin roams about . . . Peter
reading . . .*

Sally
So.
California?

Robin
Sunny.
Money.
Funny.

Peter
How's the Work?

Robin
Tiptop, Dad.
Very hard. Very intense. Very challenging.

Sally
Still 'in love' with it?

Robin
Passionately.
Nagy-Wellcome Lecture.

Sally
On?

Robin
Structure and Image Systems of . . .

Sally
Casablanca . . .

Peter
Your mother's favourite film . . .

Sally/Robin (*mock amazement*)
No?????

Peter (*quoting badly*)
. . . 'Play it again, Sam . . .'

Sally/Robin exchange glances of pity and derision . . .

Robin
it isn't actually '*again*' . . . Dad . . . it's just . . . 'Play It,
Sam . . .'

Sally puts a hand on his arm, shakes her head . . .

They all wait . . . Robin comes and sits close to Sally.

Robin (*whispering, furious*)
He can quote the whole
of English Literature from *Gammer Gurton's Needle*

to *Rape of The Lock* . . . but he can't watch a fucking
film with proper *attention* . . .

Sally (*fairly good impersonation from . . .*)
Liebchen . . .

Robin (*perfect impersonation from* Casablanca)
. . . here speaking American for practice . . .

Sally
. . . darling sweetheart head . . .
What watch?

Robin (*looking at his watch*)
Ten watch. (*Sighs.*)

Waits . . .

Sally
Love life?

Robin
Nada.

Sally
Sex life?

Robin
Panda.
You?

Grace appears . . . it is earlier . . .

Grace
I called.
Your ansaphone.

Left a message.
You'll call when you get in, I thought.
I leave another message.
I'll be reading in bed.
Call me when you get in.

Three o'clock I wake up. . . .
This is so humiliating and clichéd
my brain's turning into some kind of *Chocolate*!
Beginning to get the picture here
beginning to understand the subtext . . .
I lie in bed arguing with myself that you've
got in but you were too *drunk* to listen
to your messages or you're too *nice* to wake
me up so late but I *know* you're not that nice
you're somewhere
Making Whoopee
Hay
Creating . . . *Schism* . . . no matter how I argue
against myself on your behalf . . . for your sweet
nature for your loving constancy
I know that although there's no *phone*
message from you there's one Big Cosmic
Message . . .

*Grace swears to herself fulsomely in her own language
as light on her fades into . . .*

Sally
We're on a break.

Not liking it. Robin sees. Face and body sympathise . . .

Why?

*Grace and Sally, from their separate places, conduct a
parallel rant at each other . . .*

Sally
I've got a lot to deal with, alright?

Grace
I *know*.
But.
Time's Wingèd Chariot.
I love you.

Sally

Ugh. Don't. Don't.

Grace looks.

In parallel . . . big big rant . . .

Grace

You know what . . .
I think you're right . . .
It might not work.
I mean . . . we don't want to endure the
heart-rending embarrassment of a *perverse* ceremony
do we? No!
I mean . . . we have to look ahead!
Expect disaster!
Keep a lookout for *problems*!
I mean . . . the future can only be *bleak*, yes?
I mean . . . you might *get ill* . . .
I might get ill . . . Ah! . . . so no point
getting into anything when people might get *ill*!

Sally

Love! What's that? Free care!
Custodial! Regulations.
And . . . Bother!
And *two* people like . . . *coupled*
like a . . . *chain* . . . chains! . . . it's
concave . . . not . . . convex . . .
looks *in*
not   *out*
can that be the way to . . .?
shouldn't it . . . *free* . . .?
not . . . tie *down* . . . pin *down* . . .
'Let the winds of heaven blow between you!'
Rejoice in what we've got!
Grace!
Rejoice!

Can't it . . . we . . . stay?
Doesn't doing something to . . . *fix* it . . .
Change it?

Until . . .

I don't understand you!

Grace
I understand you.
I understand you.
Coward.

Sally
There's few things to . . . (*She mimes ironing . . .*)

Robin takes her hand. Looks at it . . .

Robin
Your hands are getting just like . . . Mum's

Sally tries to take her hand away. Robin resists.
A slapping match. Funny. It subsides.

Sally
Heard from Julie?

Robin
Christmas.

Sally
How's Tom and Sophie?

Robin takes some photographs out of his wallet . . .
hands them one by one to Sally . . .

Robin
Good . . . good.

Sally
This is still in Greece . . .?

Robin
Kalkidiki . . .

Sally

So she's still with . . . Costas?

Robin

No. But that's okay apparently.

Sally

Well . . . they're nice and brown, anyway . . .

Robin

As soon as they can . . .
He's twenty . . . she's eighteen . . .
they become more and more curious
about me . . .
they track me down . . .
I'm older but well-preserved.
Kevin Costner's playing me.

Sally

Nice.
But he'll never capture your
impenetrable depths . . .

Robin shrugs . . .

Robin

It's heart-stopping at first . . .
that moment when they come upon me . . .
de-barnacling my sea-going boat . . .
and there's many individual and group
scenes where they hurl recriminations
and hurt at my head . . .

Sally

But you keep a gritty silence about their
mother's behaviour . . . because under that
craggy, beachbum exterior . . . you're a
gentleman . . .

Robin
. . . and . . . slowly . . . achingly . . . they soften
towards me . . .

Sally
they want a ride on the fucking boat . . .

Robin
first . . . the girl . . .
then . . . oh so reluctantly . . .
the boy . . .

Sally
They love him in the end.

Robin nods. Sally puts her arms round him.

Waves crash.
Seagulls.
Magnificent sunset . . .

EIGHTEEN
A MAGNIFICENT SUNSET

Peter washes Evelyn's face with a flannel as . . .

Peter
Darling
We need to discuss something . . .
I've   put the house on the market . . .

*Evelyn responds only to the ministrations of the
flannel . . .*

Evelyn
erf . . .

Peter
well   it's   the size
and the money freed up would be handy for . . .

He indicates 'all this' . . .

and
there's a flat I've had a look at . . .

Evelyn
na . . .

Peter
very handy for the A437 so I
can zoom up here in twenty-three minutes
in decent traffic density . . .
Cliveden Road   so
and   view over the eighth and ninth greens!
You've always said I live at the bloody Golf
Club anyway . . .
anyway
I've talked it over with those two
and
well, Robin's not keen but you know how he
loves that house . . . but Sally thinks go for it . . .

Evelyn
Bucket!

Peter
Make everything . . .
easier to manage
efficiency-wise
for whatever happens
and
I hope it's alright with you

Evelyn

darling

NINETEEN
A MURDER SCENARIO

Sally
Honestly
We're waiting for her to die.

Just . . .

Visiting the ruins until

Set us free

Catapult us into the next . . .

Him on his own

More on his own

More   with . . . (*her*)

Shakes her head.

Anyway . . .
think about that *tomorrow*, Scarlett!

To Robin . . .

Go on . . .

Robin is thinking deeply . . .

Robin
It's set in a society where euthanasia is
punishable by *death* . . .

Sally
. . . Kind of death?

Robin
The worst kind.

Sally

Boredom.

Robin

Yeah . . . Dad's the main executioner . . . you
get strapped into a chair . . . he does his Golfing
Triumphs

Sally

or his Courtly Love in Medieval Literature . . .

Robin

until you . . . (*die*) . . . it doesn't *matter*
. . . the scenario '*il scenario*' is the *mother* has to be
murdered by the children . . .

Sally

. . . it's a bit fucking *Freudian* . . .

Robin

Archetypal. Mythic Dimensions . . .
to save their father
from . . . wearing himself out, dying and leaving
the children . . .

Sally

poor fucking *orphans* . . .

Robin

ex-*actly* . . . but the children have to commit the
perfect murder.

Sally

So they get away with it.

Robin

Clean away.

Sally

Okay.

They both think long and hard . . .

Sally

We can't go for the obvious . . .
the stealthy pillow over the sleeping face . . .?

Robin

Dull. Been done. Don't you think?

Sally agrees physically.
 Evelyn wakes up . . . speaks to somewhere . . . not someone . . .

Evelyn

its colours
its with a lot of about
oh
where do you live
where are you
are you?

Robin

Should be something *devilishly fiendishly* clever . . .

Sally

who's our audience sympathy with?

Evelyn

There's a!!!!
Isn't it. . . .

She points to her ear . . . indistinct noise in it.

(*very indignant*) I think she might have *said* something!

Sally touches her mother gently, distracted . . .

Evelyn (*appears to be thinking very deeply . . .*)
I'm pretty sure it was a *Tuesday* . . .

Robin

Okay.
The very clever brother has a workshop like
Ryan O'Neal's in *The Driver* . . .
he's a firearms expert . . .

他's a perfectionist
he's an inventor . . .

Evelyn
No, no
my *brown* leather handbag!
ttt!
ttt!
Ttt!
(*disbelieving contempt*) . . . I mean . . . *really*!

Sally
What's the dull sister doing . . .?

Robin
She's looking after her mother . . . establishing a
caring facade . . . while the very clever brother
perfects . . . a bullet made of . . . *ice*!

Sally
Ice?

Evelyn (*laughing delight* . . .)
. . . one of them had just a dab of white fur here (*chest*)
like a little *cravat*!

Robin
And the caring sister comes in . . .
fires the ice bullet throught the mother's brain . . .
kills her . . .
then it *melts*!
The evidence is thus . . . destroyed!

Sally
Leaving only the dull sister at the scene of the crime . . .

with the *gun*!

Robin
Damn!

an ice *gun*?

Evelyn
    Give me that
    give me that . . .

    Screws up an imaginary, tiny piece of paper.

    Thank you!

Sally
    Lose the gun.

Robin
    Yes.

Sally
    Lose he's a firearms expert . . .

Robin
    Well . . .

Sally
    Keep he's a perfectionist . . .
    but make him a really wussy nerdy
    anorak . . .

Robin
    Oh . . .

Sally
    Keep the ice. Keep the workshop. But he mends *clocks*.
    Keep the caring sister facade. Nerdy brother makes an
    ice *darning* needle. Caring sister brings it in in her
        lapel . . .
    takes it out . . . (*Stabs.*) . . . through the . . . some hole
        here . . .
    Done. Murder Weapon is disappeared by The Body
    it has murdered.
    No evidence.

Robin
    Final shot. Designer gear . . . posh hotel terrace.
    They've inherited.

Sally
No one suspects?

Robin
Oh, they *suspect* . . . but they can't
prove anything.

They rest. A job well done.

Evelyn
ttt! (*disapproval*)

ma . . . (*explanatory*)

sfa . . . (*remembers*)

ce   (*yes, that was it*)

ce   (*yes, simple, that was it . . .*)

She sits very still . . . as . . .

Sally
So
a steady trudge
through ever thicker and thicker mud

*A Casablanca-style map with a white dash-line
moving across it, slower and slower . . .*

Robin (*his dramatic voice-over accent*)
across the mile upon mile
of bleak and featureless terrain . . .
the waiting
the prison
the dread terror of a no-man's land
trying to obtain the exit veezayx
to a state of complete indifference . . .

TWENTY
A STATE OF COMPLETE INDIFFERENCE

Peter sees Evelyn, Evelyn stands.
 She is mewing with distress, rather like a kitten . . .

Peter
What is it?
Evelyn?
Darling?
What's wrong?

Evelyn
mewwww!

Sally
Mum?

She feels her mother, checks her out . . . physically . . .

She's wet herself.
Dad . . .

Peter goes for . . .

Robin . . . cloth . . . through there . . .

Robin goes for . . .

Did you have a little accident . . .?

*Peter comes back with clothes, large incontinence
nappy . . . Robin with flannel, etc . . .*

Robin
Shouldn't we get someone . . .?

Sally (*mock stern*)
We rellies are *encouraged* to
help . . .

Robin

Oh God.

Sees the incontinence pad.

Oh my God!

Sally

Quite. Brace yourself . . . she's not keen
on this . . .

*She isn't. Changing and washing Evelyn is quite a
team effort. Sally is adept, Peter less so, Robin
hopeless but willing and squeamish. Evelyn mews,
complains physically and vocally, wanders off when
possible. All together now . . . this is the 'fight
sequence' . . . the three of them start off serious,
but . . .*

Fuck!
Dad . . . she's heading off!
Stand still, Mum stand . . .
no . . . hold her . . . she'll make a noise . . . but she's
just . . .
one leg . . .

Robin (*same time*)

Here!
Here!
Here!
look . . . I'll hold . . .
look . . . I'll hold . . . no, look . . . I'll hold . . .
here . . . I've got it . . .
okay . . . I've got it . . .

okay . . . I've got it . . .

Peter (*same time*)

. . . She would hate this . . . Sally! . . .

hated being seen nude . . . Robin! . . . your mother . . .

such a degrading Sal! . . . no, darling . . . Robi . . .

Sally, pass me . . .

Robin, get me that . . .

*Half way through, exhausted, they drop their guard.
Evelyn wanders off . . .*

Rolly! . . . Sabin! . . . she's off again . . .

*They start laughing . . . reluctantly . . . then in the
next stage . . . a lot . . . until, by the end . . . all three
are laughing . . .*

Robin (*all old jokes*)
I'll head her off at the pass, Kimo Sabe . . .!

Peter
No . . . you stay here, I'll surround her!

Sally
It is a far, far better thing we do now,
than we have ever done!

*Following speeches at once . . . Evelyn is enjoying
herself. Laughing delightedly . . .*

Sally
Now . . . just need to hold her steady while we . . .
now . . . weather eye out weather eye out for . . . *see*!
now . . . steady as she blows steady as she . . .
now . . . now stop . . . now . . . it's not funny . . .
now stop! Janet Reger! . . .
now . . . she needs to *step* into . . .
now . . . now . . .
Now!

Peter
Look what I've brought you, Darling?
A present!
Look . . . lovely!
Lingerie!

Beautiful!
Janet Reger!
Gorgeous!

Robin

Okay. On the case. Up to speed now.

Up to speed.
Roll cameras.
. . . *and* action! . . . it's okay . . . we can cut it . . .
we can tighten it up . . .
I've got it! Okay! I've got it!

*The task is completed. Their wife/mother is changed
and dry. Evelyn wears the kingfisher blue dress, no
shoes. All four sit exhausted in a row of chairs . . . all
four panting, smiling.*

*As their breathing returns to normal, Evelyn gets the
hiccups. This makes them all laugh again. Peter
fetches water for his wife. She won't drink.*

*They stop smiling. Evelyn falls asleep. The others watch
her. Peter pats her hand, her head . . . and goes . . .*

*Sally brings forward the dark navy court shoes, not
the black, fits them on her mother's feet as . . .*

Sally

I suppose at the end of the day . . . Jimmy . . .
A wedding's about . . .
some notion of
unconditionality . . .

Grace appears. Flowers and a whoopee cushion.

Grace
Thought I'd make the first move.
Be consistent.

Flowers.

For your mother.

Whoopee cushion.

For you.
Thought you could do with a laugh . . .

Sally
My mother's actually not . . .
she's
in a state of complete indifference.

Grace
Is she?
Are you?
. . . you look like the robber's dog . . .

Sally
Thank you.
Your colloquial English is really coming on . . .

Grace
Thank you.

Sally
Might as well give it a go . . .

Not talking about the book idea but . . .

Something fucking *concrete*!

TWENTY-TWO
MEETING THE FAMILY

Into . . .

Sally
Dad . . . this is Grace.

My brother Robin.

As Grace, Robin and Peter stickily shake hands, greet:

and this is the relative formerly known as
'Mum'

Grace
Hello, Doctor Swan.

Sally
This is Grace.

Evelyn is quite inert.

Grace gives Evelyn the flowers. No response.

Sally
Barely eating now
barely   there

Robin
you know in the first beat Rick and Elsa
are in love . . . and the whole story is gonna be
about Love versus Duty . . .

Bergman is always starlit
Bogart too.
They're special.
Their Love is . . .
They are apart . . . but somehow . . .
the light connects them . . .

Evelyn remains inert.

Sally . . . the whoopee cushion . . .

Sally (*brings out the whoopee cushion . . .*)
Do you remember this?
Evelyn?
Mum?

Sally blows up the whoopee cushion. Demonstrates it.

Evelyn looks at Grace.

Evelyn
Beautiful!

She is alight with love.
    Sally sings 'The Look of Love'.
    Robin and Peter throw confetti.

TWENTY-THREE
A PHOTOGRAPHIC MEMORY

*All five are in separate spaces. Fog starts to roll in about
them . . . each is lit . . .*

Sally
A wedding story.

She is holding the hat she described earlier . . .

Grace
I got married.
I got married.
I got married.

Sally
I was finally true to my gene pool . . .

Peter
I didn't go into details at The Golf Club.

Just said 'I'm taking Evelyn to see Sally.
She's having a bit of a party'
I say 'She's A Career Girl!'
Both my children are . . . it's their Careers
that are most important to them.
Grace. *Lovely* Girl.
But . . .
and this business about them having *children* . . .

It's too horrendous to think about now . . .

Grace
I found this *Humanist* minister to bless the union.

Sally
Danish! (*of course!*)

Peter (*shaking his head throughout this* . . .)
Woman minister!
Humanist!
Purple sort of outfit.
Very nice speaking voice though
Very clear in all the . . . / confusion

Sally
It really has a happy ending, this story.
Don't kid yourself
Weddings are *always* about Family!
My mum *did* come to my wedding.
I *did* get married.
A small affair
bizarre
odd
unreligious

Peter
Some of the *people* . . .

Sally
unblessed

two women . . .
she'd have *hated* it . . .
Half way through the best woman's speech . . .

Peter
Dear me!

Robin
Mum farted.

Sally
Great big wet loud fart.

Grace
Everyone paused . . .

Sally
What to do? Pretend nothing had happened.
Concorde had just flown over?
Mum decided for us.

Robin
Mum . . . smiled.

Sally
Actually . . . it wasn't just a fart . . .
it was actually a very big, satisfying shit.
My mum's never been good with cream.

Peter
Darling!
Evelyn!
Darling!

*Sally is grinning, Peter is grinning . . . as the light
fades on her . . .*

Robin
We're in the hangar
it's a cold night
chilly for Casablanca . . .

an old plane . . .
it doesn't look like it can *taxi*
let alone *fly* . . .

Sally (*disapproving*)
This metaphor . . .!!!!

Robin
Fog
Fog everywhere . . .
the last scene at the airport is where they all *escape*
and the Good go off to fight Bad . . .

whether
on foot
by auto . . .
or plane . . .
everyone finally gets some sort of
exit-veezays . . .
it's where everyone *flies* . . .

The light fades slowly.

The End.